The Men'

by

Juan Garcia
&
Joe Pellegrino

The Men's Struggle Cycle
© 2020 Juan Garcia & Joe Pellegrino

All rights reserved. No part of this book may be reproduced, stored in a retrieval system, or transmitted in any form or by any means without expressed written permission of the authors.

All scripture references unless otherwise noted are from the HOLY BIBLE, NEW INTERNATIONAL VERSION®. Copyright © 1973, 1978, 1984 by International Bible Society. Used by permission of Zondervan Publishing House. All rights reserved.

Edited by Raun Barretto
Cover graphics by Joe Pellegrino, Jr.

ISBN-13: 978-1546740162
ISBN-10: 1546740163

Legacy Minded Men ™

We would like to dedicate this book to our families who love us, our friends who support us and our Lord who saved us!

-Juan and Joe

Introduction

You're probably wondering what this book is all about. Well it's definitely not your average book for men, that's for sure. It is designed to make us think. For example, isn't it interesting that many physiological changes women go through have the word "men" in it? You know, **men**struation, **men**opause, etc. We wanted to draw your attention to this by giving you a perspective that would not only stick with you but will help provide you with a dual understanding.

Here's the skinny – there is a lot in common between a woman's menstrual cycle and a man's struggle cycle. Yes, you heard us right. To make sure, let me repeat that statement; there is a lot in common between a woman's menstrual cycle and a man's struggle cycle. A scriptural example of what we mean by the men's struggle cycle is found in James 1:12-15 (NIV) which says:

[12] Blessed is the man who perseveres under trial, because when he has stood the test, he will receive the crown of life that God has promised to those who love him. [13] When tempted, no one should say, "God is tempting me." For God cannot be tempted by evil, nor does he tempt anyone; [14] but each one is tempted when, by his own evil desire, he is dragged away and enticed. [15] Then, after desire has conceived, it gives birth to sin; and sin, when it is full-grown, gives birth to death.

Therefore, we thought it would be helpful to make an in-depth breakdown of how these two compare as it relates to the cycles.

To do this we will use the Apostle Peter as an example. Also please understand as you read the stories in this book, they are predominantly flowing from me, Juan Garcia, unless otherwise noted.

Are you ready for this? Let's go!

Overview

As we introduce this concept, we are reminded of the birth of the organization named Legacy Minded Men back in 2009. My co-author, Joe Pellegrino, had a vision that was born out of an understanding that men had declined in their God given role of leader. What a painful yet rewarding process! In fact, Joe preaches that the greatest problem in the world is not abortion, sex trafficking, drug/alcohol abuse, corrupt governments or even terrorism. They are merely the byproduct of the real issue which is men who have abdicated their role as leaders, husbands and fathers. That IS the CORE issue!

You see, the mission of Legacy Minded Men is to: transform lives by engaging, equipping and encouraging men to build a **Christ-centered** legacy. This is no small task, as men have grown complacent and desensitized to their true calling.

Through the process, now some years later, we have noticed certain cycles; both positive and negative. For example, on the positive side there is a gentleman on our team who has overcome persistent patterns of serious sin to become a great asset to the ministry of Legacy Minded Men.

On the negative side, there are guys who get excited about possibilities and/or opportunities...things get going and then, CRASH! – the pressures of life get to us, we become isolated and thus block our potential in the process of seeing what could AND should be birthed.

Therefore, there is a correlation between the men's struggle cycle and, don't laugh ladies, the cycle women go through, which has within it great purpose. Let's explore!

What is a Cycle?

To begin with we need to define the word cycle. A cycle is an interval of time during which a characteristic, often regularly repeated event or sequence of events, occurs.[1] My hope is that as men, we can identify the struggle cycle that operates within us and ultimately affects our everyday lives. There is a pattern of behavior that launches us into the cycle of which we find ourselves struggling. By studying the patterns of a woman's menstrual cycle, you can almost predict its arrival. Sounds crazy, but it's TRUE! In fact, this book will help you see how the signs are all there for us to identify the struggle cycle we fall into AND understand what we need to do to control it.

In order to understand phases and cycles men struggle with, I believe it would be helpful to see the phases and cycles women go through as their bodies prepare to be in a position of producing new life. For

---

[1] http://www.thefreedictionary.com/cycle

example, we as men can struggle with such things as pornography, procrastination, relational conflicts and anger to name a few. Here's a quick synopsis:

Premenstrual Syndrome (PMS)

This is a preparation phase giving the body a warning as to what's to come. The byproduct of this phase can produce bloating, moodiness, cramping, irritability and things that just make the body uncomfortable. But remember, it is serving as a warning because a lot is going on inside, although you don't necessarily see it on the outside (besides maybe some acne). This phase is widely known as PMS.

The Menstrual Phase (Menstruation)

The menstrual phase is the part commonly referred to as "the period." The official start of the cycle is the first day of the menstrual phase – the inaugural day of the period. This is known as the Follicular Phase. Menstrual blood is shed from the lining of the uterus. It goes from the uterus through the cervix, vagina and out through the vaginal opening.

A period usually lasts about three to seven days. It may seem like more, but the average amount of menstrual flow for the entire period is about a quarter of a cup!

The Follicular Phase

This phase is all about the body preparing for pregnancy each month. It starts with the estrogen hormone telling the lining of the uterus to thicken and develop to prepare for a fertilized egg. At the same time, another hormone, known as the follicle-stimulating hormone (FSH), stimulates the ovarian follicles to grow. Each follicle contains an egg. Usually, one egg will get totally ready for fertilization each month.

The estrogen levels rise dramatically during the days before ovulation and peak about one day before the next phase starts. Bottom line guys, this is what affects a woman's emotions.

The Ovulation Phase

This surge in estrogen triggers a spike in a third hormone – the luteinizing hormone, or LH. LH is what makes a follicle rupture and release an egg. If a female has a regular 28-day menstrual cycle, ovulation usually occurs on day 14. However, most women have different menstrual cycle lengths. In general, ovulation happens 11 to 16 days before the upcoming period.

Ovulation is what it's called when one of the ovaries releases a mature egg. The egg travels out of the ovary, into the nearest fallopian tube and into the uterus. As the egg moves down the fallopian tube over several days, the lining of the uterus continues to grow thicker and thicker. It takes about three to four days for the egg to travel toward the uterus. From there, an egg waits for about 24 hours in hopes of being fertilized before it starts degenerating.

The Luteal Phase

After ovulation, the luteal phase begins. The empty follicle turns into a corpus luteum. The cells of the corpus luteum produce estrogen and large amounts of progesterone. Progesterone stimulates the uterine lining to prepare for a fertilized egg.

Here's where two things can happen. If she becomes pregnant, the egg moves into the uterus and attaches to the lining. If she is not pregnant, the lining of the uterus is shed through the vaginal opening. The period starts and a new menstrual cycle begins.[2]

I know that's a lot of information, but now you know what our women go through month-in and month-out. The value in this information is to know what they are going through as it relates to empathy and the power of the process. It also serves as a direct lesson for us to see that cycles have phases that we should be aware of (see James 1:12-15). This will

---

[2]   http://www.always.com/en-us/tips-and-advice/your-first-period/your-menstrual-cycle-phases

help us identify our struggle for what it is and be prepared for it.

IMPORTANT: This book does not subscribe to the idea that we are not to struggle anymore as men. However, we cannot change what we don't confront; and we cannot confront what we don't identify. Once we are aware of the cycle we struggle with, we can forge a better plan to overcome obstacles that prevent us from being the men that we've been created to be; men of ACTION, men of PURPOSE!

As we dive into the next pages, keep in mind the constant cycle we find ourselves in. What will it take to embrace the cycle? How can I pay more attention to the patterns and habits that have been formed? Am I the man I've always wanted to be? The man I was created to be? These questions will be answered as we identify the **men's struggle cycle**.

Stage I: PMS – Pre-Men's Struggle

I absolutely love sports! Ever since I can remember, I've been intrigued by the competitive nature in sports. In my opinion, there's a drive that doesn't exist in any other industry in the world like playing sports. It's the ultimate challenge to become better, prove yourself to yourself and others of how competent you are in a particular sport. It also can show you what you lack in terms of the things that it takes to be a winner or a champion. This all comes with preparation.

I have a profound respect for the game of football. It has taught me discipline, how to be part of a team, hard work and sacrifice. The game itself, I believe, is won during the week not on game day. When I played, I took that very seriously. As we would prepare for our opponent, I would internalize as much as I could about the different sets and schemes that team could throw at us. It was during our practices that I really learned how to enjoy the game because it caused me to prepare at a high level and I was committed to leaving all I had worked for throughout the week, on the field. I was one of those weird guys that was actually pumped when it came to practice. My teammates at first hated my enthusiasm because they dreaded practice. But when they saw my commitment and heart left on the field, they respected me for it.

As a musician, I also love music. Although I look forward to an actual performance, I am part of a small percentage that actually enjoys rehearsals. I love brainstorming ideas for cuts, stops, solos, etc. It really helps to develop a fluid chemistry with other band members and makes the sound flow better. Plus, we get to jam without being limited to a program, so cool!

In both illustrations above, you can see that talent and skill can only take you so far in the game of life. We must be committed to the moments that prepare us for what's to come. Whether it's a career, a family, a business move, whatever it may be, you can only succeed in it if you have gone hard during 'practice' or the preparation phase. As men we cannot underestimate the power of practice. It is where we can see what we are becoming to fully experience being the men we were created to be.

Now let's look at the other side of this.

When I (Joe) was a kid I was a very good baseball player and I knew it. I loved power and being able to hit the ball hard. I loved being the number 3 or 4 hitter. I just loved playing the game! But that was the problem. I loved playing the game, but practice was for the guys who had less talent. I felt I could easily get by on my raw talent but the term raw, in and of itself, speaks to something that still needs development.

I received a rude awakening when I got to high school and a lot of the "less talented" guys were shooting past me. Why? Because they put effort into their practice, not just showing up for the game unprepared like me!

As you can see, in order to gain results, we cannot underestimate the power and importance of preparation/practice. When we are intentional about pursuing our goals and dreams, they push us forward. Let's be clear, they do not come about automatically. There will be times of frustration and even the desire to quit or not give your best effort. But if we persist, persevere, and have the right attitude, hard work will *always* pay off. As a close friend always reminds me, "trust the process".

So how does this relate to a woman's menstrual cycle? Let's start with PMS.

What is PMS?

PMS (as it is known within the female menstrual cycle) stands for premenstrual syndrome. This is the _preparation_ period, no pun intended, and occurs before the woman goes through the actual cycle. It is a warning that something will happen soon, so you better be ready. Symptoms appear before their period starts (as many as five days) and will disappear during the period. Symptoms can affect their bodies *AND* their brains, and their intensity can vary quite a bit from girl to girl. (As if they don't have enough to deal with!).[3]

You know one of the things that I don't like to hear in professional sports is when the media, players and even coaches refer to the preseason as "just preseason". Really? You mean preparing for the season is not a big deal or not important? Well excuse me for preparing but if I want to be the best athlete I can be, I am going to make sure that I prepare well so that when the "real" season begins, I'm at an advantage in my sport. It is not "just preseason". It is preparation for what's to come – the inevitable.

When a woman is experiencing PMS, her body is reminding her to be prepared. So, as men, when we are in the pre-men's struggle phase, we must be mindful of the need to be prepared for what's to come. As individuals we have a responsibility to prepare and be ready to go. But ultimately, our lack of preparation not only affects us, but our whole team (family, business, etc.) as well. The warning signs are a way for us to also recognize our need for strong relationships.

Speaking of preparation, this reminds me so much of the life of the Apostle Peter in so many ways. After

---

[3] http://www.always.com/en-us/tips-and-advice/your-first-period/what-is-pms

Peter learned quite a few things about his faith, he wrote a couple of letters to followers of Jesus. In his first letter, chapter 5 verse 8, he gives an analogy of how we should always be prepared.

1 Peter 5:8 (NIV)

[8] Be self-controlled and alert. Your enemy the devil prowls around like a roaring lion looking for someone to devour.

I believe he is also writing out of his own experience. Remember when Jesus was crucified and Peter had denied knowing his friend; not once, not twice but three times? He wasn't prepared; so, he writes about being vigilant.

The word vigilant can be defined as being on the alert, as for danger or error; watchful. Sometimes we can become so desensitized and not realize when danger is lurking right around the corner. Being watchful keeps our spirit man on edge, which will cause our focus to be heightened. We can then be like a house alarm with sensors; any slight movement that is not normal will cause it to go off.

Peter also makes the comparison of the enemy, who seeks whom to devour, to that of a roaring lion. This is a pretty interesting choice of analogy because Jesus is known as the Lion of the tribe of Judah. So, from one lion to another, the enemy tries to mimic that of which Jesus truly is – a powerful lion. The interesting part of this is that scientists have discovered that lions usually don't roar when trying to devour their prey. If they roar, it would alert their potential prey and provide them with a head start to get away. Furthermore, they say that lions only roar when they are old and missing teeth. They do this because they do not have the strength to intimidate their prey. So, instead, they roar to intimidate the prey, which makes them feel powerful and once again provides them with a perceived edge.

This is a great reminder to us as men that, in preparation, we should not be easily intimidated by the things that appear to be powerful or threatening. Whether it's an addiction, failed relationship, ruined career, tainted reputation or anything appearing insurmountable, our defender Jesus is not "like" an empty roaring lion. He *IS* the Lion of the tribe of Judah who is not only for us, but also with us…always! Remember that we prepare for the battle, even though we know that the war has already been won. The fight is fixed, so to speak. The preparation is to help us grow in the areas necessary and learn more about ourselves as we learn to respond to situations of adversity and not react. After all, fear is a tactic of the enemy; don't give in!! Instead understand that fear is actually (F)alse (E)vidence (A)ppearing (R)eal. This realization in itself, is a game changer!

There is a difference between responding and reacting to a situation. When we react, the very word in and of itself says it – act! Every act brings with it drama. What I mean by drama is those reactions that sometimes come with tantrums, fits of rage, child-like attitudes we may display to show how unhappy we are with what's happening. We don't need any more drama in our lives. But when we respond, this entails a process in which we filter our emotions and our thought process to determine what would be the best outcome. We respond accordingly because we have taken the time to weigh the consequences of our decision.

Warning Signs

If you've driven a car long enough, you probably experienced a time when a light goes off in the dashboard. Yes - it's the check engine light. Ugh - so annoying. This light serves a purpose. It is there to alert the motorist that the time has come to check the maintenance of the vehicle. The light, for the most part, is designed to continue to either alert with a 'bing' or stay on consistently until the maintenance requested has been completed. The temptation many people experience with this is that of ignoring the light. Well, that will not fix the problem. It will only prolong the inevitable. So, this 'annoying' light gives us an opportunity to prepare some time to take the vehicle, get its maintenance taken care of, and fix the issue. The more we ignore the light, the more susceptible we will be to have a serious problem with the vehicle. It is a warning sign and it allows us to prepare for it. We must face the issue and deal with it. Ignoring it is not an option. We must confront it and go on offense to get it done.

Offense keeps us forging ahead. ***When we fail to plan, we plan to fail***. Therefore, having an offensive plan will enable us to not only be responsive in a healthy way, but proactive. It will also help put us in the best position to analyze where we are in the process of the cycle. As a coach of both boys and men, I can see a pattern that develops which inevitably leads them to getting into trouble. These patterns are usually unbeknownst to them because, as men, we are not usually taught to prepare or to have a focus during "preseason" so that we can maximize our "regular season" approach. We find ourselves in the midst of a mess and wonder;

"How could I have prevented this?"

"How did I get here?"

"What just happened?"

Many women, not all, complain about having cramps during PMS. This is an ultimate warning sign that the body releases to prepare for what's to come. Others complain of bloating, irritability and even pain. These are all signs to be mindful of so that all the necessary preparation should now take place. It means that any day now, the body will menstruate. For men, this is the phase in our lives we need to be sensitive to warning signs that we may be tempted in different areas of our lives.

For some men, it is working long hours, not enough rest, high stress levels or fear. Our bodies have ways of communicating to us when these, and other examples, are moving us to the point where it can be harmful. We must be so focused during the "preseason" or PMS that we see it clearly. If we don't adjust accordingly, something or someone will suffer the consequences of our choices. Do you see it?

James talks about this:

James 4:7 (NIV)

[7] Submit yourselves, then, to God. Resist the devil, and he will flee from you.

Even when we feel we are powerless in those situations James reminds us to simply submit ourselves to our creator. He's got our back. In order for this to occur we need to know who He is and what His word says. Why? So we can claim it!

Submitting ourselves speaks of a willingness to yield, voluntarily, to an outside thing; in this case - God. This can be extremely difficult for us because we are wired for conquering. Our very nature as men is to lead, obtain and be victorious. Submitting is more foreign to us than we want to admit. Therefore, we are pressed again to be mindful of yet another component to our lives - yielding. But not to just yielding to anything; but yielding to the person of the Holy Spirit. He has been given to the follower of Jesus to guide us to do what God has called us to do. He knows all things and sees all things; therefore, He is more than qualified to give us the instructions we need to take the right path and make the best decision(s) needed for any given circumstance.

Keep in mind, yielding is very different than stopping. As we drive down the street of any given town or city, we will encounter both stop signs and yield signs. The stop sign is clearly saying that we must come to a complete stop before continuing down the road. The yield sign is saying to continue going along the road cautiously, considering other vehicles that may be present in the pathway. In other words, we continue on our road in life, considering the leading of the Holy Spirit who wants to show us the way and empower us along the way; but He comes alongside of us. He doesn't just "tell us what to do". He is a gentleman, so to speak, and illuminates the way as we continue in complete surrender and trust in Him. But make no mistake, we must do our part, reading the signs and being men of action. We need to prepare.

When I use the word 'prepare', I mean to make

ready beforehand for a specific purpose, as for an event or occasion.[4] In other words, there is something I know is coming and I am not going to be surprised when it comes. I'm not going to allow it to throw me off and affect my world to where it becomes upside down. I am going to do my due diligence to embrace it, resist it or decline it because of the implications within it. I always say that preparation is the best defensive weapon; and if you are a sports fan, you know the saying that 'defense wins championships!'

That reminds me of a particular NFL team from the 80's; the Chicago Bears. The 1985 Chicago Bears season was their 66th regular season and 16th postseason completed in the National Football League (NFL). The Bears entered 1985 looking to improve on their 10-win 6 loss record from 1984 and advance further than the NFC Championship Game, where they lost to the 15-win, 1 loss San Francisco 49ers. Not only did the Bears improve on that record, they put together one of the greatest seasons in NFL history.

The Bears won fifteen games, as the 49ers had the year before, and won their first twelve before losing. The Bears' defense was ranked first in the league and only allowed 198 total points (an average of 12.4 points per game). They won the NFC Central Division

---

[4] http://www.thefreedictionary.com/prepare

by seven games over the second-place Green Bay Packers and earned the NFC's top seed while securing home field advantage throughout the playoffs at Soldier Field. In their two playoff games against the New York Giants and Los Angeles Rams, the Bears outscored their opponents 45–0 and became the first team to record back-to-back playoff shutouts. Then, in Super Bowl XX in New Orleans against the New England Patriots, the Bears set several more records. First, their 46 points broke the record that had been set by the Los Angeles Raiders in 1984 and tied by the 49ers the following year with 38. Their 36-point margin of victory topped the 29-point margin that the Raiders had put up in Super Bowl XVIII which stood as a record until the 49ers won Super Bowl XXIV, also in New Orleans, by 45 points over the Denver Broncos. It was the Bears' first NFL World Championship title since 1963.[5]

What I am trying to say with this sports analogy is that, in order for us as men to experience victory in every area of our lives, we must first look for the warning signs that come to us in life. Then - prepare for the inevitable which is where victory is actually won.

Focus *"Daniel San"*

In the preparation phase, the idea is to have a better

---

[5] https://en.wikipedia.org/wiki/1985_Chicago_Bears_season

focus so we can have great clarity during the process. Remember the classic movie of the 80's, *"The Karate Kid"*? Mr. Miyagi was a great trainer and wanted his student Daniel to be prepared for the fight. Well, Daniel didn't really see the value in the mundane tasks that his sensei required of him. Daniel wanted to dive right into the moves, the kicks and basically kicking butt. However, there's wisdom with experience and Mr. Miyagi knew what Daniel needed, to be prepared for the ultimate showdown, which by the way, did not just prepare him for "a" fight but for a LIFETIME.

Think of the preparation phase or PMS as the "wax on, wax off" part of the whole process. Although it seems meaningless and even trivial, it is the ultimate preparation for a lifetime. When we do something over and over again, it becomes a habit.

This connects directly to the basic spiritual disciplines that are essential to victory, such as prayer and daily reading of Scripture. Without having a consistent pattern of applying these disciplines (again, think of "wax on, wax off"), the success and happiness that we all desire in life will elude us. We will be spiritually weak, and as a result be susceptible to the negative cycles that we all struggle with. The Master said that we must "seek first the Kingdom of God" (Matthew 6:33). When we make seeking of God a priority and not an add-on, we have developed the perfect offensive strategy!

Also, if we allow someone to show us or help us in the process (life coach, coach or mentor) we are held accountable and maximize our learning during the preparation phase. It is all about having a game plan to win. And I know we all want to win in life!

Remember, we are not born winners or losers; we are born choosers! Make no mistake, who you are at this moment is the summation of all the choices you have made to date. Not happy about where you are? No problem! Make better, wiser choices!

Irregularities

One of the realities of the PMS process is that not all women go through it on a consistent basis. There are females that will go months without these warning signs, which causes one of two things: concern or relief. Concern can be good and bad; good in the sense that it can make one super sensitive to the signs as they begin to show up. Bad because it can produce anxiety and a sense of unrest, always expecting the worst.

One thing is for sure, irregularities keep you on your toes. There are those times when you are feeling pretty good about yourself, your primary relationships are healthy and all of the sudden, an old girlfriend messages you or an old friend hits you up asking you to hang out when you know it's not a good idea. Then they proceed to give you a guilt trip trying to convince you to hang out or they raise the question, "what kind of Christian are you"? Be aware and stay focused! You can do it!

Preparing is essential and will always be important for anything we look forward to in life. As we close this section on preparation, let us prepare our hearts and minds for the 2nd stage of this cycle that challenges us all. Are you ready?

Questions to Consider

What are some of the warning signs prior to your specific temptation(s)?

_____

_____

_____

_____

_____

_____

_____

_____

What are some of the everyday habits you've been taught?

_____

_____

_____

_____

_____

_____

_____

How have they helped?

_____

_____

_____

_____

_____

What's cramping you up? Is it anger? Bitterness? Resentment? Fear? Loneliness or something else?

_____

_____

_____

_____

_____

_____

How can you become more sensitive and aware during the time you experience "PMS"?

_____

_____

_____

_____

_____

_____

_____

Remember: *It is better to suffer through the pain and uncomfortableness during the preseason than to be vulnerable to a season-ending or worse off, career-ending injury during the regular season.*

Stage 2: Period? – Use a P.A.D.

The Menstrual Phase (Menstruation)

We have prepared our hearts and our minds, and now we are ready to go. In the Overview we provided you with a quick look at The Menstruation phase. Let's go a bit deeper.

How does this connect with the struggle that men face on a constant basis? Well, it does in many ways, related to those moments in a man's life where there's a potential to produce life – speak positive words – but is tempted instead to speak down to that person. Opportunity missed and you are left with a hurt individual and potentially a life thrown off course.

Remember, life is in the blood, so the blood is a sign of life or something life giving. When we as men, are given an opportunity to speak into the lives of others, we can potentially speak life – flow of blood – or speak death. That is why there are many out and about living like the "Walking Dead"; they are alive but not living; merely existing. This is usually a result of a man speaking down to others – i.e. "you're an idiot", "you'll never amount to anything", "you're such a stupid ass", "when are you going to learn", "be a man!" etc.

This may not be limited to words, but it can also include gestures or actions. I remember when I was in high school, my football varsity coach told me there were a few college scouts interested in meeting my parents. I was excited and nervous at the same time. Excited because I had an opportunity to potentially play football in college and nervous because my parents were not my biggest fans. My mother suggested that sport would pull me away from my faith in Christ and my father, well - let's just say he was a good absentee dad; he was still in the family but was always absent. He had no clue I even played football.

Well one afternoon, a college rep visited our home and was sharing with my mom all the benefits of why we should consider their school. My mom just sat there and nodded her head, as to say, "yeah ok, but my son needs to focus on his spiritual life". After all, my mom believed that I had a call to ministry and football was potentially a distraction. As we are sitting in the living room in conversation with the rep, my dad arrives at the house. He walks into the living room and right away, it is obvious he is drunk. It is only 4pm. He asks about this meeting of which he was not aware of and my mom tries to keep him calm, or at least from embarrassing us all. Once my mom told him that I had an opportunity to play football in college for free, the next gesture, not a phrase, that came out of my dad's mouth, would hurt me for years to come without realizing it. My dad looks at me, looks at my mom, then looks at the college rep; waves his hands at me as to dismiss the whole situation and snarls, "ahhhhhhh". This was to suggest, "oh whatever". This broke my spirit and even my soon-to-develop manhood. Words and gestures matter!!!

These type words are killing the souls of so many in our society, especially our youth. This is why kids grow up with a chip on their shoulder. After all, **hurt people hurt people**!

So what do you do when there's a period? You use a pad. Well, for our purposes you use a P.A.D. which stands for a Paternal Affirmative Dialogue. What I mean by Paternal Affirmative dialogue is the need every male has to receive affirmation from another man he respects. This affirmation is not limited to words that are spoken over the male. This P.A.D. also represents a position of spiritual authority that we as men have been given by God to serve as priests. I am a strong believer in the power of a man's affirmation. The man represents the head of the home. Therefore, it is imperative that the man is intentional about having an affirmative dialogue to stop the proverbial bleeding! We must speak life into the lives of those around us; especially those we love and are entrusted with. There is no compromise in this. We need to put a P.A.D. on the period.

We stop the bleeding by allowing ourselves to be held accountable by other men. There is an overwhelming need for truth-telling and accountability in every sector. The bleeding or issues of life, as we call it, dress themselves as temptations that we face. As we surround ourselves with good men that hold us accountable and disciple us, we put a P.A.D. on the bleeding - the issues!

As I speak in different parts of the U.S. as well as other countries, I get to meet a lot of great people. I have also had the opportunity to meet men, both young and old, that are incarcerated. It is so sad to hear their stories, not just about the reason they are locked up, but about their terrible or non-existing relationships with their fathers. The numbers are mind boggling. Here are some statistics that break my heart and I hope you take the time to really read them:

Statistics[6]

- 63% of youth suicides are from fatherless homes (US Dept. Of Health/Census) – 5 times the average.
- 90% of all homeless and runaway children are from fatherless homes – 32 times the average.
- 85% of all children who show behavior disorders come from fatherless homes – 20

---

[6] https://thefatherlessgeneration.wordpress.com/statistics/

times the average. (Center for Disease Control)

- 80% of rapists with anger problems come from fatherless homes −14 times the average. (Justice & Behavior, Vol 14, p. 403-26)
- 71% of all high school dropouts come from fatherless homes − 9 times the average. (National Principals Association Report)

Recent policies encourage the development of programs designed to improve the economic status of low-income nonresident fathers and the financial and emotional support provided to their children. This brief synopsis provides ten key lessons from several important early responsible fatherhood initiatives that were developed and implemented during the 1990s and early 2000s. Formal evaluations of these earlier fatherhood efforts have been completed making this an opportune time to step back and assess what has been learned and how to build on the early programs' successes and challenges. While the following statistics are formidable, the Responsible Fatherhood research literature generally supports the claim that a loving and nurturing father improves outcomes for children, families and communities.

- Children with involved, loving fathers are significantly more likely to do well in school, have healthy self-esteem, exhibit empathy and prosocial behavior, and avoid high-risk behaviors such as drug use, truancy, and criminal activity compared to children who have uninvolved fathers.

- Studies on parent-child relationships and child wellbeing show that a father's love is an important factor in predicting the social, emotional, and cognitive development and functioning of children and young adults.

- 24 million children (34 percent) live absent of their biological father.

- Nearly 20 million children (27 percent) live in single-parent homes.

- 43 percent of first marriages dissolve within fifteen years; about 60 percent of divorcing couples have children; and approximately one million children each year experience the divorce of their parents.

- Fathers who live with their children are more likely to have a close, enduring relationship with their children than those who do not.

- Compared to children born within marriage, children born to cohabiting parents are three times as likely to experience father absence, and children born to unmarried, non-cohabiting parents are four times as likely to live in a father-absent home.

- About 40 percent of children in father-absent homes have not seen their father at all during the past year; 26 percent of absent fathers live in a different state than their children;

and 50 percent of children living absent their father have never set foot in their father's home.

- Children who live absent their biological fathers are, on average, at least two to three times more likely to be poor, to use drugs, to experience educational, health, emotional and behavioral problems, to be victims of child abuse, and to engage in criminal behavior than their peers who live with their married, biological (or adoptive) parents.
- From 1995 to 2000, the proportion of children living in single-parent homes slightly declined, while the proportion of children living with two married parents remained stable.

Stop the Bleeding

So how do we stop the 'bleeding'? We need more fathers to step up and have **P**aternal **A**ffirmative **D**ialogue with their children and also with their wives/girlfriends. We also need mentors, uncles, grandfathers, coaches, etc. to have these Paternal Affirmative Dialogues as well, especially if a father is not in the picture. It is all about a man, affirming their children, mentees, players, significant others, utilizing P.A.D. that will surely stop the bleeding that's so negatively affecting our society.

Let's go back to Peter's life. There is so much in his

life we can glean from, both his ups and downs. The good, the bad and the real ugly. They all help us learn important things about how we can grow in our process of being affirming as well as receiving affirmation.

Peter is often criticized for being quick to react instead of taking some time to respond (remember we talked about the difference before?). This is because of Peter's personality. He is a go getter, a type "A" kind of guy. His intentions were good, but he didn't always consider the consequences. There is one instance in his life's story where his eagerness was actually a good thing.

In Matthew chapter 14 verses 28–31, the writer shares a story where Jesus and his disciples are crossing the lake. Around 3:00 in the morning, Jesus comes to them walking on water. Obviously, they freak out (I think I would too!) and begin to say that it is a ghost. Jesus tells them not to be afraid; that it is He. Peter, being the go getter that he was, says to Jesus, "if it is you, Lord, tell me to come to you on the water". Well Jesus probably took that as a challenge (maybe not) and said to Peter, "come". Peter of course, went and began to walk on water. Did you hear me? Peter began to WALK ON WATER! That's crazy!! He was able to experience a supernatural, miraculous and unforgettable experience with Jesus. He actually believed he could do this…or did he?

The next part of the story is the struggle Peter, and most men deal with on a regular basis. Peter took his eyes off of Jesus and focused on the challenge of the storm that was upon them. Peter began to sink in the midst of the storm. His faith was challenged, and he couldn't see himself overcome it. What strikes me as odd in this is that Peter was a fisherman by trade. Surely, he knew how to swim! But it is also an example of being overwhelmed by the storms of life. Even the simplest things we are used to doing seem impossible. Through it all, Jesus stayed with Peter and reminded him that he wasn't alone. Peter didn't need to doubt. He was in good hands. Jesus affirmed him and told Peter to simply trust him.

It is also important to note that Peter was the ONLY one who actually got out of the boat!!! He trusted, quickly moved his trust to circumstances and was once again rescued by the one he first trusted. All the while the others we mere observers. Using P.A.D. requires action, even if our actions result in mistakes. The important thing is to learn from those mistakes and get back in the game by grabbing hold of the Master's hand.

Another instance of Peter's life was recorded in the book of John chapter 16. Here we see Jesus sharing with the disciples his nearing death. This is a somber and very emotional time for Jesus as he is dealing with the inevitable; the cross. As Jesus is sharing the news, Peter jumps up and begins to say how this cannot and will not happen. Peter was willing to die in Jesus' place (or so he thought) and began to say how this was not about to happen. But Jesus, knowing Peter's struggle with his mouth and trying to say the right things in life, rebukes Peter. He confronts his thinking, **not his personality**. He begins to tell Peter what we are trying to convey in this chapter. Be prepared; be alert. Just because it may feel like the right thing to say doesn't mean it is necessary. Jesus reminds Peter, in an *affirmative* way, that God's plan will prevail over our plans.

There was also the time Jesus was getting arrested in the garden of Gethsemane. The Roman soldiers came upon Jesus, with the disciples near him, and approached him to arrest him – as told in the book of John chapter 18. Peter immediately and under compulsion (reacting) jumped up and cut off the ear of one soldier. As the saying goes, "OMG!" What a scene straight out of a movie! His intentions are true, but his demonstration is way off. Jesus, again, must talk to Peter and remind him of God's plan. He affirms him and continues to love on him.

Jesus took every opportunity to teach Peter the lesson he needed to learn to grow. He continued to challenge Peter in meeting his needs. At one point, Jesus was teaching his disciples the importance of being servants at heart and did so by washing their feet. This was a big lesson because in first century

Jewish culture, men's feet would be really dirty from walking all day and night in sandals. Every time they would come to someone's home, they had to take off their sandals at the door and wash their feet. Jesus showed the disciples the ultimate act of service by taking it upon himself to wash their feet.

Peter, once again, reacted by telling Jesus he was not worthy of his feet being washed by him. It was well intended but he was missing the point. Jesus had to affirm Peter and remind him of another life lesson about God's plan but did it with affirmation. Jesus was intentional about having constant Paternal Affirming Dialogues with Peter knowing that this would eventually stop the bleeding of Peter's outbreaks. This is the only thing that will stop the cultural bleeding we are all experiencing out of the lives of individuals, and in particular men, that have lacked this type of P.A.D. in their lives.

This is not something that costs money to solve; but if not solved costs money. It is a moral imperative for men all over the world to begin to have affirmative dialogue with those they love and start a revolution of affirmation. Just imagine yourself sitting in a chair with your eyes closed. All of a sudden, your father is standing behind you with his hands on your shoulders and whispers gently in each ear, "you matter to me", "you are worth it", and/or "I love you just the way you are". How would that impact you? Will it make a difference? There is power in affirmation, particularly paternal affirmation. My challenge to you in this book is to dare to be intentional about affirming someone you love, especially your children. It will impact the culture, society and ultimately the world!

We have prepared to be the best that we can be in Stage 1 and we have been challenged to stop the proverbial bleeding in Stage 2. Now let's dig into the results of our hard work in Stage 3.

Questions to Consider

What is (was) your relationship with your father?

_____
_____
_____
_____
_____
_____
_____
_____
_____
_____
_____
_____
_____
_____
_____

What is (was) your relationship with your children?
(if applicable)

_____

_____

_____

_____

_____

_____

_____

_____

_____

_____

_____

_____

_____

_____

Are you willing to stop the bleeding by using a
P.A.D.?

_____

_____

_____

_____

_____

_____

_____

_____

What will it take for you to start today?

_____

_____

_____

_____

_____

_____

_____

Do you have a man in your life that can affirm you? If not, are you willing to find one?

_____

_____

_____

_____

_____

_____

_____

Remember: *Our words create worlds. What we say has the power to construct or destruct. The choice is ours to allow the bleed-out or stop the bleeding by using a P.A.D.*

Stage 3: Prepared for New Life

My intent, thus far, has been to take you on a journey from a pre-, during, and post aspect **of our Men's Struggle Cycle**. We dealt with the warning signs that prepared us to be at our best when the time came. All of this leads us to an end result. There is a principle that no one can escape. It is the principle of sowing and reaping. All of creation exists in obedience to this principle. Whatever action we choose to take, there is an inherent consequence, whether it is good or bad. Let's look first into the end phase of the women's menstrual cycle.

When a woman has conceived, her body prepares for new life. She is carrying the potential of something, better yet someONE new. New life! There is a bloodline in her that details a pattern as it relates to individuals. It is a direct result or production of the intimacy of individuals. This intimacy is validated the moment the woman is ovulating. Again, ovulation is the time in the woman's monthly cycle where one of the ovaries releases a mature egg. The egg travels out of the ovary, into the nearest fallopian tube and finally into her uterus. As the egg moves down the fallopian tube over several days, the lining of the uterus continues to grow thicker and thicker.

It takes about three to four days for the egg to travel toward the uterus. From there, an egg waits for about 24 hours in hopes of being fertilized before it starts degenerating.

If the female wants to reproduce, this is a pivotal time because it is ideal for a pregnancy to occur. And we all know that a pregnancy (assuming good health) is the promise of new life, the birth of a child. This is the ultimate sign of new beginnings and where another human being is formed. That is a visual for what a pedigree looks like. (In the section on 'Profession', we will explain more about our particular usage of the word "pedigree"). What an amazing opportunity to witness new life!! It is the greatest miracle given to us on earth – the ability to procreate.

Production

We are a direct result of a man and a woman's reproductive abilities; albeit together through intimacy or through other medical procedures such as in vitro fertilization. We refer to this result of the birthing process as "Production". My wife always says that all babies are pretty much the same when they are born. They are usually placed in the nursery, tightly wrapped in a blanket with a small cap on their head. Some cry more than others, but they are all defenseless, in need of love and being nurtured. When you see them in the nursery, you cannot determine which will be scientists, doctors, lawyers, ministers, athletes, criminals or president of the United States (coincidental order). They are all the production of 2 people and carry their own D.N.A. They also have their own fingerprints that distinguish them from everyone else – both those living and dead. Each has their own identity even though they are the production of 2 individuals. This is what makes them who they are as individuals, completely unique.

Process

There comes a time when they are given a clean bill of health, along with mom if applicable, and the baby is ready to go home. This is when they are cared for and provided for in all sorts of different ways. Some get a lot of love; others don't get enough and still others sadly receive none. But the production now enters a phase of process. The production aspect of their existence will always apply but the process will ultimately be visible to all in different ways. There comes a time where they may "look" like their parents physically and even do things similarly, but the process will show who or what has influence over them as they manifest out what goes into them. Without the production aspect of their lives, they would not exist. But without the process, they would not be who they are. So, what about the proverbial question who was first – the chicken or the egg? We all know that production was first. At the same time, it's the process that "makes" us who we are. The question is, who do we resemble: our producers or our processor(s)?

Simon or Peter?

When we look back at Peter's life, we can pinpoint the moment Jesus changed his name. In actuality, the intent was to change his identity. Simon was his birth name which was Hebrew and meant 'listen'; but Peter was his name in Greek (derived from the Latin) which means rock or stone. What Jesus was trying to tell Peter was that he was going to be processed in order to become who he was created to be.

This wasn't an overnight process (just like babies take time to grow and develop), but it sure was meaningful. We discussed some of Peter's shortfalls or stumbles. But we later see in John 21 that Jesus comes back to have breakfast with Peter and the disciples, and he affirms Peter. He asks Peter, "do you love me?", as to say, "are you still willing to be processed?" This was an affirmation of love from Jesus, since Peter had denied him when he was being crucified.

Then in Acts 2, after the 120 or so are gathered in the upper room during Pentecost, they are all filled with the Holy Spirit. They go on to share the experience with all who would listen. It is Peter who delivers the first sermon at a mass gathering. After his 2nd sermon, thousands upon thousands make decisions to follow Jesus. This is Peter's redemption from his past failings, and a sign of him receiving his affirmation from Jesus. Jesus protected Peter for the process he needed to experience, in order for him to be the man he had been created to be.

Fallopian Tubes?

First of all, I love saying fallopian! Ok, now seriously, the fallopian tubes have a very important function. They serve as a protective gateway for the egg that the ovaries release, sending it through to get to the uterus. This is a very important part of the process so the egg has the ability to be fertilized, which in turn produces the eventual baby or new life. So when we talk about the child being processed or going through a process in life with those responsible for them, think of the home being a giant fallopian tube serving as a safe-way or gateway where it is to be protected for optimum fertilization or ability for life itself. The problem is that there are times when the fallopian tube(s) gets clogged or pus develops which creates blockage; not allowing the egg to flow. How many of these babies (who will grow to be children) end up in homes where their destiny is blocked? They are not affirmed, loved, cared for or given the best opportunity of new life.

We must be more proactive as men to prepare the best environment where healthy growth and development can occur. We are responsible on many levels. Remember that the egg when it gets to the uterus, is waiting to be fertilized. Who or what is it waiting for? You - the man! The one carrying the seed that once planted, fertilizes and gives the egg the opportunity to develop. It is our responsibility to do what needs to be done for this to happen in the healthiest way. We carry the ability to fertilize so that an egg can receive its full identity, true purpose and the lineage can continue. In the environment we are to provide, we have the choice to either set the temperature or be thermometers. One creates while the other measures. One sets the standard while the other seeks to know what the standard is. We cannot do both. The lives entrusted to us depend on us more than we realize. The same way plants or flowers depend on us to water and nurture them; those we are connected to depend on us for the same.

Profession

The word profession is usually recognized when used to describe a job or career. In this section, I would like to use the word for another definition it carries: an act or instance of professing; a declaration; an avowal of faith or belief; a faith or belief.

Someone once said (a very cool carpenter around 30 A.D.) that out of the abundance of the heart, the mouth will speak. What that means is that we will ultimately say or profess that which we are full of or that which we have believed. Here's the reality; there are things that we are full of that may not be positive but because we've believed it, they are in us. There comes a time where whatever is in us will come out. It will literally flow out of our mouths in what we say because we have put enough faith or belief in it that it is a part of us.

There are things we've been told, whether growing up in the home or at school or by friends at some point in our lives, that we've never dealt with. We've allowed those words to infect us to the point where we believed them. Eventually we gave those words credit, enough for them to stay in us. As we grow and develop relationships, there are situations that will provoke those beliefs to flow out of us in word and at times through anger, which can lead to violence. That's when we in turn sow seeds of anger and hate into others and we bypass the production pedigree and create a new pedigree of people marked by our hurtful words. Once again, "hurt people, hurt people". A truer statement you will not find.

When I use the word 'pedigree' here, what I mean is bloodline or what someone is made of. This word has been used to describe the descent of an animal. However, that is not the only way it is used. It can also apply to describe someone's ancestry, bloodline or lineage. In a psycho-spiritual sense of the word (which is how I am using it here) it refers to the makeup of someone because of what they learned; either through nature or nurture.

In other words, I am of Puerto Rican descent. My father is Puerto Rican and his father was Puerto Rican, and that is our background/pedigree. But when it relates to pedigree here, my father is an alcoholic and his father was an alcoholic. So, my pedigree should have been one of an alcoholic...BUT GOD! I have made the choice, by the grace of God, to create an environment not only for myself, but for my children and my children's children, to change the narrative and be who God created us to be.

There comes a time when we must be honest with ourselves and determine whether we have been:

- true to our productive pedigree
- introduced to a different pedigree
- and/or if we have created our own pedigree based on our environment.

This introspection will help make sure those we are in relationship with receive a healthy dose of affirmation, love, and protection to know their true pedigree. As you saw in the statistics discussed in the previous chapter, there is a pedigree of males in particular, that have been introduced to an environment of lack, prison, dysfunction, limited thinking, low self-esteem, depression, violence, crime, neglect, and so much more. They are hurting and in great need of knowing their true pedigree because for most of them, their 'fallopian tubes' had a blockage that prevented them from being the best they could be.

Power

As a man, what do you think about when you hear the word power? Is it might? Is it strength? These are examples of it but when defined, it means "the ability or capacity to act or do something effectively". At times what we think is the meaning of something, turns out to be a very limited view of what that word or thing really means. As men, we have the ability to treat others well and develop strong, nurturing relationships with those we love. We have a tremendous opportunity to produce a pedigree that enables others to be empowered and perpetuate the process. But in order to make that happen we need to be men of action!

What does a man of action look like? My co-author, Joe Pellegrino, along with my friend Jack Redmond, wrote a book called *"Transformed: 7 Pillars of a Legacy Minded Man"*. In it they lay out what a godly man, a legacy minded man truly looks like.

We have to remember that Jesus didn't only come to save us from our sins. He came so that we could, through His divine power, build a new and different life in Him. Having said that all men must ask themselves two simple, yet powerful questions.

1. What foundation am I building my life on?

2.   What is my game plan to win in life and build my legacy?

Transformed begins by talking about building the strongest foundation possible. That is the foundation of Jesus Christ! There is no stronger foundation.

By building on the foundation of Christ you will begin the process of discovering your true identity and that will point you to the purpose for which you were created.

Whether building a house or even stronger muscles, it requires time, energy and a plan. *Transformed* then gives a 7-step plan, built on the proper foundation, to win in life and to build a strong legacy for generations to come. Once understood AND put into action, these 7 Pillars will be the game plan that leads to success.

The 7 Pillars are:

Pillar 1: PRAYER

Prayer strengthens your relationship with God, creating two-way communication with your creator!

Pillar 2: PERSONA

Persona is who we really are. This process looks at our character and integrity as well as our relationships.

Pillar 3: PURITY

Purity maintains an unbroken relationship with God as your leader. So many men fall here, not just sexually but also through justification.

Pillar 4: PURPOSE

Purpose begins to come into focus once we align ourselves under God's leadership and maintaining the 3 previous pillars.

Pillar 5: PRIORITIES

Priorities bring focus to live out your purpose. The old saying goes "when we fail to plan, we plan to fail". Nothing can be truer! A God given purpose deserves an excellent plan of execution.

Pillar 6: PERSEVERANCE

Perseverance pushes you to never give up. Make no mistake. The devil is real and does not want to see you living out your purpose. New level, new devil! Fight through it!

Pillar 7: POWER

Power is unleashed through the "uncapping" of the Holy Spirit, who resides in all that have claimed Christ as Savior. This power, the same power that raised Jesus from the dead, is fully released as you live out the first 6 pillars.

Bottom line: Don't live without a strategy. Focusing on these pillars built on the firm and powerful foundation of Christ, will help you become a legacy minded man, a man of God, and will result in a life of lasting impact. If you choose to be transformed today, you can discover the victory God has for you tomorrow!

Questions to Consider

Who are you....*Really*?

_____
_____
_____
_____
_____
_____
_____

Do you have your own identity or are you the creation of others?

_____
_____
_____
_____
_____
_____
_____
_____

How do you exercise your power?

_____
_____
_____
_____
_____
_____
_____

How do you respond during your struggle?

_____
_____
_____
_____
_____
_____
_____

What do you believe about yourself?

_____
_____
_____
_____
_____
_____
_____

Remember: _Most men are simply a product of their environment; their original pedigree. But you can change your pedigree to your true pedigree if it is not in line with the man you were created to be._

Epilogue - Bringing it all Together

Let's summarize.

Gentlemen, we are in a war. But this war is not like those that are fought on the battlefields of this world. This is a spiritual war. That is why we must be vigilant and self-aware to all the warning signs (Stage 1 - pre-men's struggle) that serve as an indication of what's to come. How we prepare in this stage by recognizing the warning signs, will be indicative of how we respond to the next phase.

If we study first responders, like firefighters as an example, a lot of their time is spent waiting for something to happen. Well, as men, something will always happen. Things such as addictions, rough relationships, hardships, overwhelming quotas to meet, parenting and of course health issues, are things that 'happen'. When they happen, they cannot catch us off guard. We must have a P.A.D. (Stage 2 - stop the bleeding) ready to apply to the issues of life. We have to stop the bleeding using the P.A.D. that represents accountability, affirmation and discipline. Now that we have the P.A.D. in place, our spiritual man will be equipped for the next phase - the ability to experience new birth.

As we respond in a healthy way to these issues, we position ourselves, by the grace of God, to expect new life; not only in us but out of us (Stage 3 - new life). What I mean is, we will immediately impact the next generation in a positive way because of the legacy minded choices we've made. Ultimately, what we sow we will surely reap.

So, let's do better. If you are currently doing your best, I salute you and your family thanks you. We can always do better. This is a struggle cycle we find ourselves in. Just like the menstrual cycle, there are warning signs we must be aware of so that we are not caught off guard when in the middle of a mess. We must do better when it comes to being real about the patterns we have created that get us into trouble. We all have weaknesses; but we also have strengths.

As long as we know our weaknesses and have them before us, our strengths will have the opportunity needed to flourish and allow us to be the men that we have been created to be. Social media cannot do our job for us. Television cannot do our job for us. Sports cannot replace the responsibility we have been entrusted with. Remember that we are the carriers of the seeds that when sown, have the potential to multiply according to its own kind. It carries the DNA and pedigree it was designed to have for a distinct purpose.

We literally have the power to change the environment that affects society and of course the world. What a responsibility! But responsibility would not be given to those that are incapable of carrying it out. We have what it takes. You have what it takes. Just as we carry the seeds to be planted, we too are seeds ourselves. And in order for a seed to have the capacity to multiply it must first be buried and die. During its burial, it goes through a germination process. In reality, it is not dead; it is dormant or sleeping. It is seeking to anchor its roots so that in due time, when it is called upon to break out and flourish, it is grounded.

We must die to ourselves, metaphorically speaking, and give life to those relationships we care about. There is no magic potion; no lottery ticket that can do this. It is hard, intentional work that brings with it the best reward life can give which is, other people finding their purpose in life because of the environment we've created for them. We have the great privilege to make deposits in the lives of those we care about and see the production become the new life that gives them the power to be successful. There is too much bleeding out and life is being lost.

We have an opportunity to respond and not react – the difference is in the word act. Whenever there's "act" there's drama. So, responding is the opportunity to take it all in and filter out accordingly so we can pour out what's inside of us, good stuff. **Together we can encourage each other and be the men that we are destined to be.** You are not a deadbeat. You are not an idiot. You are not a jerk. You are not a mistake. You are not what has been said about you in a hateful way.

You are a man destined for greatness with the ability to change the world! Be encouraged! **Now DO IT!**

NOTES:

Appendix 1: Statistics

<u>Father Factor in Education</u> – Fatherless children are twice as likely to drop out of school.

- Children with Fathers who are involved are 40% less likely to repeat a grade in school.
- Children with Fathers who are involved are 70% less likely to drop out of school.
- Children with Fathers who are involved are more likely to get A's in school.
- Children with Fathers who are involved are more likely to enjoy school and engage in extracurricular activities.
- 75% of all adolescent patients in chemical abuse centers come from fatherless homes – 10 times the average.

<u>Father Factor in Drug and Alcohol Abuse</u> – Researchers at Columbia University found that children living in two-parent households with a poor relationship with their father are 68% more likely to smoke, drink, or use drugs compared to all teens in two-parent households. Teens in single mother households are at a 30% higher risk than those in two-parent households.

- 70% of youths in state-operated institutions come from fatherless homes – 9 times the average. (U.S. Dept. of Justice, Sept. 1988)
- 85% of all youths in prison come from fatherless homes – 20 times the average.

(Fulton Co. Georgia, Texas Dept. of Correction)

<u>Father Factor in Incarceration</u> – Even after controlling for income, youths in father-absent households still had significantly higher odds of incarceration than those in mother-father families. Youths who never had a father in the household experienced the highest odds. A 2002 Department of Justice survey of 7,000 inmates revealed that 39% of jail inmates lived in mother-only households. Approximately forty-six percent of jail inmates in 2002 had a previously incarcerated family member. One-fifth experienced a father in prison or jail.

<u>Father Factor in Crime</u> – A study of 109 juvenile offenders indicated that family structure significantly predicts delinquency. Adolescents, particularly boys, in single-parent families were at higher risk of status, property and person delinquencies. Moreover, students attending schools with a high proportion of children of single parents are also at risk. A study of 13,986 women in prison showed that more than half grew up without their father. Forty-two percent grew up in a single-mother household and sixteen percent lived with neither parent

<u>Father Factor in Child Abuse</u> – Compared to living with both parents, living in a single-parent home doubles the risk that a child will suffer physical, emotional, or educational neglect. The overall rate of

child abuse and neglect in single-parent households is 27.3 children per 1,000, whereas the rate of overall maltreatment in two-parent households is 15.5 per 1,000.

Daughters of single parents without a Father involved are 53% more likely to marry as teenagers, 711% more likely to have children as teenagers, 164% more likely to have a premarital birth and 92% more likely to get divorced themselves.

- Adolescent girls raised in a 2-parent home with involved Fathers are significantly less likely to be sexually active than girls raised without involved Fathers.
- 43% of US children live without their father [US Department of Census]
- 90% of homeless and runaway children are from fatherless homes. [US D.H.H.S., Bureau of the Census]
- 80% of rapists motivated with displaced anger come from fatherless homes. [Criminal Justice & Behavior, Vol 14, pp. 403-26, 1978]
- 71% of pregnant teenagers lack a father. [U.S. Department of Health and Human Services press release, Friday, March 26, 1999]
- 63% of youth suicides are from fatherless homes. [US D.H.H.S., Bureau of the Census]
- 85% of children who exhibit behavioral disorders come from fatherless homes. [Center for Disease Control]

- 90% of adolescent repeat arsonists live with only their mother. [Wray Herbert, "Dousing the Kindlers," Psychology Today, January 1985, p. 28]
- 71% of high school dropouts come from fatherless homes. [National Principals Association Report on the State of High Schools]
- 75% of adolescent patients in chemical abuse centers come from fatherless homes. [Rainbows for all God's Children]
- 70% of juveniles in state operated institutions have no father. [US Department of Justice, Special Report, Sept. 1988]
- 85% of youths in prisons grew up in a fatherless home. [Fulton County Georgia jail populations, Texas Department of Corrections, 1992]
- Fatherless boys and girls are twice as likely to drop out of high school; twice as likely to end up in jail; four times more likely to need help for emotional or behavioral problems. [US D.H.H.S. news release, March 26, 1999]

Census Fatherhood Statistics

- 64.3 million: Estimated number of fathers across the nation
- 26.5 million: Number of fathers who are part of married-couple families with their own

children under the age of 18. Among these fathers –

- 22 percent are raising three or more of their own children under 18 years old (among married-couple family households only).
- 2 percent live in the home of a relative or a non-relative.

- 2.5 million: Number of single fathers, up from 400,000 in 1970. Currently, among single parents living with their children, 18 percent are men. Among these fathers –
  - 8 percent are raising three or more of their own children under 18 years old.
  - 42 percent are divorced, 38 percent have never married, 16 percent are separated, and 4 percent are widowed. (The percentages of those divorced and never married are not significantly different from one another.)
  - 16 percent live in the home of a relative or a non-relative.
  - 27 percent have an annual family income of $50,000 or more.

- 85 percent: Among the 30.2 million fathers living with children younger than 18, the percentage who lived with their biological children only.

- 11 percent lived with stepchildren
- 4 percent with adopted children
- < 1 percent with foster children

ABOUT THE AUTHORS

JUAN GARCIA

Juan Garcia is a consummate professional speaker and an internationally recognized leadership development expert. He has been able to bring show stopping performances at conferences worldwide delivering evidence-based strategies that have an immediate impact. Juan has earned a reputation where high profiled celebrities and top companies trust in his leadership and life coaching skills. He has made appearances in FOX News as well as TBN NYC. He has been married to Deborah since 1996 and together have 2 children: Jordan and Hannah.

JOE PELLEGRINO

Joe Pellegrino is a men's pastor, author, speaker, certified life coach, consultant and entrepreneur. He is the President and founder of Legacy Minded Men, whose mission is to "Transform lives by engaging, equipping and encouraging men to build a Christ centered legacy". He has appeared several times on television including Fox News and TBN and been featured on many radio programs across the country speaking on men's issues. Joe is the co-author of the books Safe at Home, Transformed, That's My Dad!, 2 Words From God for the Legacy Minded Man And Fathers Say. Joe has also developed and presents several workshops and seminars. He and his wife, Bethanne, have three children and one grandchild.

RESOURCES

Download the Legacy Minded Men app

The Legacy Minded Men app allows you to keep the discussion going by providing a daily devotional, blog, training videos as well as a fresh weekly lesson...all at no cost!

To download the free app go to the App Store or Google Play and search for Legacy Minded Men

Would You Like to Host a Men's Workshop?

Legacy Minded Men provides several workshops to Engage, Equip & Encourage your men to be all that God created them to be.

Programs include:
- 360 Discipleship
- Conference on Demand

Workshops include:
- Overcoming the Men's Struggle Cycle
- Move the Chains
- The 5.5 Questions Everyone Must Answer
- Transformed: 7 Pillars of a Legacy Minded Man

For more information visit:

www.LegacyMindedMen.org

Made in the USA
Columbia, SC
27 November 2020

25664827R00039